C000136949

Petals of Love

Dofini Tamini

PublishAmerica
Baltimore

Hardcover 9781462662326
PUBLISHED BY PUBLISHAMERICA, LLLP
www.publishamerica.com
Baltimore

Printed in the United States of America

Contents

Prologue

Close your eyes; imagine. Take a deep breath and smile, meditate. Envision, look, observe; see the colors, smell the freshness of oxygen and let's take a trip to heaven.

Introduction
(The last 15 minutes)

Looking at myself in the mirror, the countdown begun, "20 minutes left to live!" And then "19 minutes left!"

Like an angel appearing and disappearing, that being was letting me know that my time had come. I used to see that same being in the past; coming and taking people away, but this time he came for me.

As a matter of fact, I remembered that kid, my friend, that one time. This kid that I knew long ago was living his last five minutes. We were together in an accident when he got hurt, but I didn't want him to go because I cared for him. It was so cold and he fell in a frozen lake. After I got him out, I told him to pray, so God would let him live and stay with me.

And he said, "I already did, but He said no, when the time is up to go, you have to go, there is nothing good left on earth for you."

So I asked him, "How much longer can you hold?"

"Five minutes, maybe." He said.

The time run out so fast, I didn't even get a chance to say goodbye, he passed away, he was only eight years old; I cried.

The rescue finally came, but it was too late for my friend; he was gone already. I was fine however, my time wasn't up yet.

They rescued me to safety and while I was sitting there, alone, I saw a kid standing by; he was standing with another kid, I do not remember the name of that other kid, but he was about two years old and well dressed. He handed me his little hand and when I shook it, he said, "Wow! It's cold!"

And I said, "Yeah! It's cold in here."

Then they both put their hands in mine and disappeared afterward. I realized then that it was my friend that came back to show me his new friend and say goodbye. He looked happy where he was. I was touched; I cried.

"15 minutes!" The being just informed me.

Still standing in front the mirror, I wondered if I'd go to heaven. I guess so, or else that creature wouldn't be here for the countdown. I remembered how others are also escorted by evil creatures when passing away to the dark side.

Yet, time is running out. I feel happy already; I'll get to see my friend in heaven, there, death will be no more.

"The time is up!" The angel said.

"Goodbye!"

Bloody red Philia

Softness of laughter

Have you ever had a dream with colorific imaging looking all sharp and crystal? If so, know that you just had a dream in HD. Don't worry about the 3D; it comes along with it.

Boys, don't try this at home; the best and fastest way to get to the moon: tell your woman in love (of you) to hold the ladder for you.

They say, "The bird in your hand is better than the one on the tree." Should we observe this in detail? What if it's "A crow in your hand" would it be better still than "The colorful parrot nesting on your tree"? Should that be a tough decision to make?

A baby cries much, but he doesn't drop as many tears as an adult in love.

Scent of life

Whoever has a dream, let him pursue it. But let him also gear himself with courage and strength, for long suffering is on the way of success.

How is it so easy for us to outlive ourselves into pleasure, but so hard to withhold ourselves for a season? Our sinful nature, I guess! So here is a little encouragement: giving up to pleasure is shameful, but preserving self for a special one is most honorable.

A good behavior is a virtue. It is very hard to cultivate, but it will change one's life as it lasts forever.

Humility will make you cry, but you shall only grow stronger. Pride will make you fall, and you shall only grow weaker.

If my hand is short, lend me yours. You might need my leg someday.

The beauty of the day is in the eye of the joyful one. But the darkness of the night obscures the vision of the sad-hearted.

How can one be entrusted with a child if he cannot bring a single project onto life?

The best treasures in life are not redeemable with money: peace, joy, love, contentment, wisdom, time, meekness, faith, strength, youth, health, sobriety, friendship, and more. These are also the treasures of heaven.

If I cry tonight, I would not want anyone to know about it. But when I smile in the morning, I want my joy to strengthen the broken-hearted.

If I make the day of 1000 people and break the heart of the 1001st, I shall not rest until peace falls upon the broken-hearted. Otherwise I shall consider my task of the day a failure.

A spiritual growth defiles the physical principals. But a physical growth is overthrown by a mightier physical power.

Yesterday is gone, and tomorrow never comes. What shall we make of the day of today; a day of joy, love, victory, success, or a day of accomplishment? Shouldn't we make good use of it while we can; since the present is what counts?

A well-spoken word would appease an angry-minded. But a good word harshly refined would rise up the anger of a calm-minded. What we say does matter, but how we say it matters the most.

Knowledge is good when wisdom and understanding add up to it; if not, success will be your downfall.

Humility is very delightful, but its cost is very painful.

A dot of dirt on a white shirt would ruin an entire cloth; that is how much a bad deed can stand out to ruin the good ones.

Joy is not an achievement. It's a state of mind.

From worse to bad might seems negative, but it's a sign of prosperity.

A need seems very little compared to a want, but it is a vital thing in one's life. If we could only be content with what we need, we would understand that joy it not so hard to accept.

In the days of the Bible no one has ever heard of such a thing as an economic crisis. They dealt with famine and other natural calamities. So why is it that we suffer much today? Should we still classify it as an evolution? Or should we refer to it as a regression since the love of money is what added more pain onto our sorrows?

You can write a heck of a story, but if no one can read it; what good is it?

Success has no recipe! It is purely a blessing!

Women, take note. Men were not created to be submissive to women. One way or another they will exercise their leadership; if they cannot get it at home, they will get it outside! So know that whenever your man bows down to you, he is plotting a diversion to cover up some of his dirty activities.

We are all special and important; even the ones who do the crappiest and/or stupidest things have their place among us; they are known to be as such and thus they receive our recognition because they bring laughter onto our hearts. Can anyone tell me how would life be like without laughter?

It's alright to give up for a season, only remember that if you do not carry it on, no one else will.

It is better sometimes to keep quiet and suck it up than to speak up and ruin the peace in the neighborhood; just a random act of unselfishness to better our livers.

Even though it might happen overnight, success never comes in one day. It is a timely process.

We often expect people to take it easy on us or to make it easy for us. Don't we forget that life itself is a challenge, designed for the strongest to survive and for the elite to make it (to heaven)!

Do not over-focus on your past failures to hinder your progress; rather learn from them and keep on stepping.

Let's walk with a winning spirit. Build and rebuild after losing everything, smile and rejoice even though things are going wrong, come and go as if we belonged nowhere, love and cry as if it were the first time we ever loved; and keep in mind that life on earth is only for a season.

Fortune is not limited to material. One can be rich without a dime in his pocket. It's a blessing. Likewise one can be miserable with a million in a bank. It's a curse, sometimes.

Do not emphasize on the upcoming promise to stress up your mind, rather look at what is being done and rejoice from it.

A fulfillment of a dream is not up to your pocket, but up to you. Look closely to what you have in your hand, you might accomplish that dream. Only if you would dare to open that eye!

Lift up your head, there is a King within you. Walk royally; you are a son of the Mighty One. Carry yourself as a King regardless of your situation; for on earth or in heaven you shall inherit a kingdom.

Do not lay eyes on the physical outcome of a project, neither rely on the benefit in it for self, but consider the impact of it on others' lives. Bring a smile or some hope to someone. It is so priceless.

Anyone capable of finding balance in any of life's circumstances should be capable of enduring the toughest life condition. Nonetheless, how can one find balance without a Pillar to lean on?

When living a great story, remember that you are not living it for yourself, but for others.

The best way to live the toughest life condition is by not considering it. Focus on the bright side of the picture instead. It will help.

Rejoice when things get tougher; when people oppress you to give up; this is the moment to keep on pushing: The blessing is near.

Go, seize your dream! Even though you quit it 1000 times, go back the 1001st time! You can still make it.

Sacrifice first and then get rewarded later.

A hard-worker will only work hard for a season; but an easy-worker shall keep on working all his life.

In the old days, they rubbed two pieces of wood together to make fire. They knew then, if they would rub them long enough it would bring forth fire. So know also that if you keep on pushing long enough your light will surely shine.

On the East coast, success is based on how much work you put in your daily business. On the West coast in revenge, success is based on how much investment you put in your dream. So, which one is best?

"Hang in there!" seems so simple, but it takes more strength to just sit still than to do something.

Do not see it as a curse when doors are being closed before you; rather see it as a sign revealing you to dig deeper in your potential.

A dream can be fulfilled without the fulfillment of your dreamed fortune. Nonetheless, be happy, because many didn't get as far as you did.

Have you ever done something that you're ashamed of or made a mistake that you're deeply regretting? If so, shake it up and move on! It happens to all of us. It is also part of our human nature.

Consider yourself lazy even though you're not; thus you'll get much work done in your life.

A good worker does not stop giving his best in only one specific position, but does the same in every position he is appointed to.

In life, you'll see the rise of the few and the fall of the many. It doesn't matter if you're among the fallen; dust up yourself and rise up again!

Those who made history are people like you and me. The only difference is that God had decided so in their lives.

Never reveal your limits to the enemy; yet, reveal them to him when you know that you can go future more, so you will take him by surprise.

Which side are you on? Are you an artist, caring less about a piece of paper, but will still make it? Or are you a scholar, all about degrees and diplomas for success? Either way, understand that you'll need the other side in your life.

Just because a genius can understand things easily doesn't mean that things come to him easily.

A genius does not decide to be a genius, but finds himself being one, and most of the time he does not know it until he's told. Likewise, he would not consider himself as a genius until others consider him as such!

Nothing seems too hard to understand; anything and everything is untreatable; furthermore, theoretically explainable. You don't know what you are or who you are, who you should relate to, to identify yourself, because you stand alone in knowledge. Yet, you're lost in the hardship of self and in the challenge of fitting somewhere you can't fit. It is complicated and easy at the same time; hard, but simple in a sense. You want to be left alone, but others are in need of your gifted hands. You wish you could rest, but your mind is in constant meditation, seeking answers or solving equations or enigmas; even in your dreams, you'll come across problems to solve! Can such a mind be explained? Can his gift be solved? What a strange mechanism for these who have been appointed to that special task, these that we call, "Geniuses"! What a life, only enjoyable if one has the Almighty alongside him.

A genius is also human, he has habits just like you have; makes mistakes just like you do, struggles with life just like you do, and bound to the human nature just as you are! Anyway, we are all the same!

Have you ever wondered how you could interpret your dreams? Well, know that there is no template to proceed in such a way; rather understand that every dream has its unique way to transmit a message, so it will be uniquely related to you. Only one key remains: Pray and ask for it!

Perfume of wisdom

A godly man is loved for his reverence to the Almighty. A worldly man is loved because of his pocket book. It is sometimes hard to make the difference; however, with time, the true face of each starts to come to light, and the true friends shall always stand, still.

We are pilgrims on earth, passing through the hardship of life to be prepared for our ethereal home. One day we breathe and on the next day we fall asleep. Naked we came and empty handed we go; not even that body that we care much about shall be brought along; yet we set our heart upon vanity instead. We stand one against the other for some profit that will be handed over to the next one. How sad!

One can have all the experience in the world, bear all the understanding of the world, and gather all the knowledge of the world; he can even be the smartest and/or the cleverest, but if he lacks the ability of choosing Good over Evil, he shall surely be lost; because knowing God is the beginning of wisdom; and wisdom is neither taught nor found, but given.

This goes unnoticed so easily, but remains so hard to practice. It takes more strength to keep a smile on, on a troublesome day, than to wear a sad face.

Stronger is the one who holds his tongue against provocations. Thus is the walk of the wise.

Weaker is the one who runs for a weapon on an outburst of anger. Thus is the walk of the weak.

Education is a good thing, but it is a waste if one does not put it to work.

Hold your peace when you're angry and then react afterward, when you've calmed down.

A sweet and soft tongue will always come out clean, even though she speaks hurtful words; because she would know how to appease the pain.

You are gifted and talented; and maybe you don't know it yet. But if you find the artist hidden within you, it shall make a King out of you.

Growth in one's life resides on how much pain he has been through; how many colors he has seen under the sun. One needs much strength to stand and not let the events affect him, but he also has to be flexible enough to learn from the hardship in order to move forward; taking one step at a time and walking godly in the midst of the ungodly.

A wise woman once told me, "When you see two persons fighting, pray for them even if you don't know them, that the LORD will settle their confrontation peaceably; lest their rumble comes your way and disturbs your peace!"

No matter how much you lose, keep on pushing. No matter how many times you fail, keep on trying, because your failures and losses will all contribute to your success.

In the parable of the prodigal son, the King could've sent his servant to go rescue his dearest son, but he rather held back. Why? Because it is best sometimes to let your loved one go in wander? Or is it because experience is worth more than money?

In life, sorrow and troubles will always follow, but joy will come on the day that you accept them – troubles and sorrow – to be part of the process of life, too.

Lesson of patience number 34: Remember that everything can wait, but nothing can be put on the next day.

Don't give up! You are going to make it better on the next round. Even then, don't give up! One day you're going to succeed.

Say it out loud: I am successful, blessed and prosperous. For those who do not believe so let them repeat it every morning until they do because belief will trigger the process of bringing it into existence.

I breathe, I exist. I'm not forgotten!

Those who would chose to suffer will suffer for a season; but these who would try to avoid suffering will suffer for a long, long time; a lifetime for some and an ever-ending-time for others.

The hard way is always the best way! The easy way always comes with a catch somehow.
Sometimes you don't need to be good at it to shine at it; just be there!

Seek out the recognition of the few over the many! Many will make your life miserable, but a few will make it lovable.

You never know how good you had it until you lose it. Hang on to yours while you still have it.

Discretion 101 (example): $10,000 in a black trash bag would slip right under your nose, unnoticed. But $10 in a black suitcase would easily catch one's attention.

Forgive and be forgiven; that is the pathway of peace; be prompt to seek the forgiveness of others so you can keep your peace. It is not easy of course, but worth it indeed.

The prison mentality tells us to excuse ourselves even when we feel innocent. We think it's a weakness, but it is the best way to be left at peace. Isn't it obvious, a slap on the other cheek?

Is the sky blue, multicolor, or transparent? Regardless of your answer, know that it can be applied to your life also. Sometimes blue when everything goes smooth, dark when things go wrong and transparent when you don't feel it at all. Yet, it all contributes to the beauty of life.

I am what I was chosen to be by being what I wanted to be. Yet, I am not what I am by my own power!

Lesson of humility: Hold your tongue, keep quiet; let your virtues, qualities and/or work speak for themselves; you, keep on walking.

Food is good for physical nurturing, but sometimes it is best to hold back and listen to what your body is telling you. Milk, juice, fish; or nothing at all, just some time off sometimes to absorb the excess of nutriment.

Sometime I would hold my tongue back not because I want to, but for the sake of tomorrow, another day. No one knows how tomorrow might be! I might despise you today; but tomorrow I might be in serious need of you!

Be fortified, hold on Him and wait for His time

One day, I became Christian and I said that it was going to be fine.

But it turns out that the worse was on the line.

Praying, worshiping and, the more I did, the more it seem like a crime.

What was wrong? I did not know, but God, may You forgive me this time.

I have tried, but no success! I have cried; but tears were only mine.

Because I'm a Christian, I had to wait! Why should one taste that wine!

Go through such pain in order to learn and grow up sometime.

A preparation process. To be a loser before the wining dime.

A partial pain in vision of an upcoming everlasting mine.

One day it will end forever; happiness, success; both combine.

The Almighty God will say, "Go! Now start your prime!"

His Word will be heard clearly like a whispering and His signs like a mime

Then you will know that the past is gone; from then on, reign and shine!

Do your thing and don't stop

You might try without success;
But it's not over yet, learn to deal with it,
Your time is yet to come!
God gives a time for suffering
But gives no limits to success.
Wait patiently for His time
And His is going to be yours.
It might not happen overnight
And the trial might seem never-ending,
But remember, "Where dreams fulfill
There is the Name of Jesus Christ." Appreciate.

I shall continue on

I found what I was meant for,
The ground that I should long for.

> All these years wasted.
> All that wisdom pasted.

I finally saw a sense in my life:
To be there and dwell there.
I normally see a fence in my life,

> But with Him, the heavens are the limit
> And the Earth is the beginning.

Speechless are you, when you wait on Him

Am I touched?
Am I sad?
Maybe just overwhelmed?

> My tears can't stop dropping,
> My heart however, is filled with happiness.
> My soul cries out for forgiveness.
> Am I worthy of such a blessing?

Do I deserve it?
I suffered long,
To be delivered from that pit.
Inconceivable, should I sing You a song?

> My tears can't stop thanking You
> And my emotions can't stop glorifying You.
> How beautiful,
> How wonderful.

Tired of homelessness

I have tried all that I could've tried, but I'm still hopeless.
I have done all that I could've done, but I'm still clueless.

Such a situation making me so powerless
Under the greed of this world so ruthless.

I am tired, but I can't give up, I am restless.
I am tired, but I can't sit down, I am aimless.

I would've liked to give up, but that way will be joyless.
I would've liked to put an end to it, but I am just
harmless.

I have to keep on moving, because it's not time yet.
I might cry tonight because the world is careless.
But it is all right, because the light has not dawned yet.
Weep bitterly while you can to purge your sadness.
But wait for that time that has not come yet.

I was somebody, but now, who cares anyways, I'm just a
homeless,
Life will go on still with another monkey in darkness.

Lightning blue Eros

Aroma of relationship

A dispute is good onto a relationship if there is understanding. It should teach one how to live together.

A good listener knows how to keep a friend. By listening he'll get to be listened to in return.

Security is a result of a healthy relationship.

Lovely feeds keep a relationship alive. But they have to be reciprocal.

A "healthy relationship" does not imply a "Trouble-free relationship" In fact many tribulations shall come. But when trouble rises, together you must stand.

In a long-lasting relationship, partners tell the truth to one another; they also admit their wrongs and rights and accept them, because we all make mistakes and no lies can ever cover up the truth.

Just because it's the truth doesn't mean that you have to say it! Just because it's the way you feel doesn't mean that you have to express it. Sometime things are not said just for the sake of the other!

In relationships, we often refer to theories and experiences when dealing with mates. It doesn't work all the time. The uniqueness of every single one of us gives us different ways of thinking, of doing things, of living life in general. Therefore, learning the ways of a mate and adjusting self accordantly should be the best way to go.

Wise is the one who sizes up a date (spiritually) before engaging into a relationship. It is like trying a cloth before buying it.

Here are a few tips for your date. First, you must know yourself and know what you need from a partner. Then set up key questions to size up your date (spiritually) and see if he/she is compatible or not; also make sure to check on his/her sincerity, past relationship (how many and why), tolerability to know if some of your vices (snoring, smoking, tattoos and so on) would not bother him/her and what he/she likes.

Always wonder about the reason behind his/her questions, because a date will never ask a question unless it matters to him/her.

Finally draw your conclusion and see if there is compatibility. If not, then let go.

Remember that it is always better to let go now than to suffer later.

Fragrance of romance

Marriage is slight compared to the bound between soul-mates. Nonetheless, let marriage be celebrated in reverence to the union.

A virgin should treasure her virginity and give it to the man who most treasures it.

Love and tear are for your heart to bear.

A good mate is hard to find, but the right one will do.

Women are not obligated to love their men. It is men's duty to drive them in love.

A soul-mate is meant to complement, but not to be the same as the other half.

Can a soul-mate be found? Maybe a little story might help:
"A young man once met a girl. But he didn't pay attention to her until a year later; they finally got together. Afterward, they both surprisingly found out that they were made one for the other; they remain together ever since."
If one does not take the time to discover the other standing next to him; his half may slip away from him even though he (or she) might have found her (or him).

Rejoice when you're heartbroken, because greater love is on the way.

I cry because I have to let you go, but I rejoice because I shall find my other half.

I don't want you to tell me that you love me when everything is all nice and dandy; instead, hold it for when everything grows worse, and then you shall show me love.

A hand-crafted nonsense is a sweet lecture to the one in love (of you). It is worth more than a thousand poems written by another.

One concept of love could be being able to say, "I love you" even though the circumstances push you to mean otherwise.

The Bible says, "Faith without action is dead." This also goes for love, "Love without proof is void."

A proof of love is seven times better than a thousand, "If you only knew how much I love you!"

A woman knows how to comfort a man's heart, but she also knows how to tear it apart.

Forgive me if I have hurt you. It only implies that you love me; and so do I.

Tomorrow, I shall rise bright and early. I shall look for my mate, "Have you seen my lover? She is that tall, and talks a lot about me. You cannot miss her; she is the one who loves everything within me including my flaws." And then I shall remember that she should be looking for me also. Promptly, I shall come back home and happily I shall find her waiting. Oh, how sweet is it to be in love?

They say, "When you get kicked by a donkey, and you kick it in return; both of you are the same." Shall we consider then,

"When you get bitten by a lover, and you bite him in return; both of you are lovers." But should we just stop there? "When he kisses you, you shall also kiss him in return."

Yellow and blue give out green. It defiles the mathematical concept of "One plus one equal two." This also stands for the concept of soul-mates; two mates combine to become one complete soul.

Anyone willing to love should also be willing to suffer, because love and pain rhyme together. Nonetheless, love shall overshadow the pain.

A sacrifice for love is greater than a verbal romance, but the combination of both gives out pure love.

A rose is to imply that I care about you; a fresh green one is to reveal the freshness of your beauty; the red fresh petals are to recall how much I think about you; a thorn on the flower is to remind you of how much I've hurt you, but the number of petals is to seek your forgiveness, and the entire action is to tell you that I love you.

Love is not a statement. It's a lifestyle.

Mother of love, mother of a child; from within you come forth stars and galaxies; and without you man's love strives with maladies. Sweetness with complexity; loveliness with harmfulness; so much struggle to explain a woman; yet we wonder how could we have done without her.

Baby-love, I thought about buying a plane and write your name on it to show you my love. But then I realized that it would've been a loss, because the paint would've worn out throughout the ages and the plane would've stopped flying. So I wrote your name in my heart instead; and there it stays forever to take us off on a never-landing journey of love.

If a woman calls a man, King; he shall call her Queen in return; because a King without a Queen is similar to a lion without teeth; he would miss something very crucial in his life.

I might not have gold or silver, but my love and care are worth more than diamonds.

A half of my heart to trade for a half of yours; thus is the trade of soul-mates.

Being through a lot of pain and suffering doesn't imply much pity for self. It only implies that one has learnt a lot on his way.

Don't thank me, tender beauty

I'm proud to call you my lady,
My sweet candy.
I'm thankful to be your honey,
Beauty pricy.
Speechless towards having you so lovely,
I picture us in the heavens to come quickly.
Exited when I think about some nights so bumpy,
I can see how much loving you makes me so happy.
So don't thank me because my love goes beyond crazy.
Don't thank me because taking care of you is my
responsibility
And don't thank me because I'll cherish you for eternity.
It's my call to love you without publicity,
So is my way of calling you "Baby".
I cannot catch the colors of the sun shining by,
But I will surely show you the color of my love so sunny.

You are just what I need, baby

When I was a kid, these dreams were so many,
I wanted a blonde with blue eyes on top of her nice body.
A tender skin to caress on so smoothly,
A kiss on her sweet lips looking so pinky,
And look on her sizzling body covered with jewelry.
It took me a youth time to realize that colors don't matter to
be lovely
Instead, from all above looking so tasty;
I have found me one who has no jewelry, a simple lady,
And I have discovered that jewelries sure looked good, but
have no womb. Not worthy.
That same one has no pinky lips, but speaks truthfully.
Her skin wasn't as tender as I thought, but strong enough to
help daily.
She is not blond, but it doesn't stop her to shine brightly!
She has no blue eyes but they can show me her love so
boldly.
Then I realize that I was deceived from my childhood, I
woke up surely.
With that special lady driven to me! How was I happy
To discover that time and scar could never alter her beauty.
I have discovered that beauty was better on the inside, but
again, even outside she is pretty.

Sorry for breaking your heart,
but I had to tell you

I have never told you,
But I have met someone, and I can't hide it anymore from
you.
Deep inside, I bear a greater love for her, but I really don't
want to harm you!
I'm in love with her and it has nothing to compare with you.
She is everything I have dreamt of! And again I'm sorry for
hurting you.
Her lips, her skin, her tenderness, her understanding, and
more; you have no clue!
She calls me sometimes and surely I see her every day! It's
hard for me too!
I can't stand it anymore; I have to let you know, so together
we'll decide what to do!
Her name does not matter; I'm going with her anyway,
maybe you should follow, too!
I think you should follow us! It will be the best thing to do,
Because the person who I'm talking about is in fact the one
reading this poem; you!

Come back and hold my hand.
Not too tight

Listen to me, Oh daughter of The Most High!
Queen in whom my heart finds delight!
Inside thy womb, stars and galaxies, heavens and light!
As it was and it is, mother of all nation smart and bright!
Listen, Oh beloved, seat not thyself up high
Because, King am I and Queen thou are in my sight!
When trouble comes and feelings go on to fight,
Forget it not my Queen; remember how much were we tight!
Thy hand in mind as a left in right!
Forget it not; I shall be thou, not just for one night!
But anytime I shall let thee come to me, I shall hold thy hand
as a knight!
For one day hearts may be dismayed, but with an act, love
shall show its might!
As same as my Father does onto me; so will I do onto thee to
walk upright.

Let's close it as harmless

It is a thing I don't like, it makes me depress.
It is a thing I don't want, it makes me stress,
But to me, and for me, I bet you, you are going to say yes!
I woke up this morning and I saw you sleeping on the
mattress,
Then I went into the living room and there was no mess.
You joined me afterward, and for a minute, I thought you
were a guess.
For so long I have known you, we have never settled for less.
Baby, let me call it, it's just never enough and I have a matter
to address,
Let's divorce, separate so I can conquer you again as wifeless
I still don't have enough of your love and I still feel it
endless
Baby I'm still in love with you as my first time, please don't
leave me hopeless,
Forget about the divorce and the separation, but let's do it
painless
Will you marry me one more time? Please don't say no! If
you do I'll be restless!

I love you cutie

Just a little touch of smile
Behind a little white of teeth
And baby I am happy.
Just a little shape of body
Behind a little look of model
And baby I am crazy.
I don't know if I ever told you,
I don't know if you ever knew it,
But forgive me if I have never said it.
Now know it, you are truly beautiful,
Prettier than a flower.
Truly speaking, baby, I mean it!
You shine like a beautiful star in the firmament.

I want to know you

Your hand in mine
Like a missing rib.
A smile to shine
With a lovely bib.

Nice have I said;
Yet, I couldn't see.
'Price have I paid;
Yet, I couldn't flee.

I just wanted more,
I was opened to you.
Yet, blinded, I had no clue.
I just wanted more.

A nice spirit in a beautiful look,
So long have I been waiting and so long is it going to be.
Stay near and get to know you; closer to you do I want to
be!
What I don't know, you'll tell me. Where I am ignorant,
you'll teach me.
But hey, am I allowed to read your book?

Just tell me, what is really happening?
I don't know, may be am I just loving?

I don't want to be a King to you

Even if I were a King,
Even if the world were to call me "king"
Still I will find no joy in my kingdom if I'm not your King.
Even if you were to respect me like a King.
Even if you were to see me as a King
And call me as King.
I will get no satisfaction in it if you do not call me "My King."
A soft voice calling me King
Is nothing to compare to your sweet tone calling me "My King."
My queen, I rejoice when you call me "Mon roi! My King",
My queen are you to me and your King do I want to be to you as a man, as a King.

Her name is April

Lately our relationship has become boring;
I have noticed the same as you did, no feeling.
Also, someone told me that love would be decreasing
In a relationship without disputes. So, yes honey, the boat is
sinking.

> Let's go for a fight,
> Do you remember that girl? I told you about her, she is
> bright,
> She is back! Remember I almost dated her and now she is
> back in my sight!
> Relax honey. It's just a "one time" thing, no future, no
> flight;

You are the one I want and I will stay with you, but for now
let's face it.
I wanted to mess around, and I did it.
She is back, I want her, I want a dispute with you so I am not
holding it.
Relax it's almost over and I'll be back to you, I mean it.

> Now listen, I know you might not like it, but hey. It's just
> a tool.
> By the time you'll be reading this poem, I'll be dating her
> near by the pool.
> Yeah, love will rise up once again, because her first name
> is April and the last is fool.

A day like yesterday to sow

A day like yesterday I was born,
Grew strong enough to blow the horn.
A day like yesterday were you born,
Grew strong enough to cook some corn.

I still remember that day, not long ago.
When I told you that I will go and in few days you'll
follow
And it was just a day like yesterday when it came time for
me to go.
So far, baby, time went by, so many days in a flow.

Am I going to see you again? I don't know,
I just wish it for a day like tomorrow.
Was it so the price of love? Was it so the way for us to show?
Was it so the weight of faithfulness? Was it so the way for us
to grow?

Least now I know, if I ever have nothing to give, not even
a flower to say so;
If I ever have nothing to make a living out of and do not
even know how.
I will have these things to count on you for, just like a
vow,
Your love and faithfulness will ensure me that I would not
be riding solo.

That makes me realize that one day, side by side, in an
eternal glow.
Living in our heavenly mansion and taking it slow,
We shall remember that day like yesterday where things were
tough on the earthly show.

I will find out

If I climb up a tree
And you are not scared of following me,
That would tell me something.

    If you have a fancy job
    Making big money
    And you are not ashamed of riding with me,
    That would tell me something.

If I eat some sardines
And you are not afraid of kissing me,
That would tell me something.

    If I wear dirty clothes
    And you are not ashamed of following me,
    That would tell me something.

If you see me in the morning,
Just when I wake up
And you are not scared of saying good morning,
That will tell me something.

    If you used to hang out with big shots
    And you are not ashamed of hanging out with me,
    That would tell me something.

If you used to eat in restaurants
And you are not ashamed of going for fast food with me,
That would tell me something.

    Combine three of the conditions above to give me a sign
    And four of them to show me that you love me.

Propose

Now I look at you and wonder,
May I touch you? Should I laugh? Should I cry?
Now give me an answer,
Will you marry me? May I hope? Should I remain happy?

If they had told me that such a beauty existed
I wouldn't believe it.
If they had told me that such a life could've been lived;
I would've denied it.

From the day I left you to this day I receive you,
Much more beauty I see in you.
From the person I left to the one I meet again in you,
Much virtue and love I share with you.

I knew I was about to meet a splendid one,
But I wasn't prepared for such a beautiful one.
I knew I was about to see a lovely one,
But I wasn't prepared for such a fiery one.

So beautiful that your steps sounds like music!
So splendid that your walk looks like dancing!
So sweet that your words flow like singing!
So soft that your skin inspires the exotic!

Your laugh is a symphony,
Not even Mozart or Beethoven knew that key!
Your hair is finer than silk,
Not even the exotic can find that milk!

A dream became true will you be to me as a wife.

And if someone ever told you that I'm lying
Just tell him that he hasn't discovered love yet!

Hear me out

Your beauty eclipses the one of another
And your virtues dwarf the ones that I encounter.

    Talking with you brings me to another level of
    communication.
    Hugging you gives me a whole new sensation

Of merging your heart to mine; to become one with you.
Kissing you stretches time beyond calculation
Of being forever linked to you; to remain one with you.

    I have discovered love with you
    And I want to learn more.
    Not because I want to, or love you,

But because I still have a lot to learn.
And if someone ever talked about a limited love
Tell him that he hasn't discovered that point of no return!

    Because an eternity of loving you
    Is a beginning of my love for you.

Love like a rose

Someone told me once:
Los Angeles is the city of Angels.
Shouldn't I think twice?

I came to L.A. and something happened.
I heard about the beauty of angels,
They neither need makeup nor jewels.
A flap of their wings would leave you marveled.

I think I saw one,
Her teeth are of the white of milk.
I think I met one,
Her hair is of the softness of silk.

I saw no wings on her,
But her voice pierced the shield of my heart!
I saw no fire on her,
But her eyes warmed the roses of my heart!

Should I talk to her? Could I?
Should I tell her how I felt? Would she listen?
Be quiet, my heart! How could I?
Can I? May I? I mean, just listen!

Did it happen that your name matches up with rose?
Should I offer you a rose or beautify you like one
decorating a flower?

Do you believe in angels?

It was dinner time, in the dining room,
This past Friday; if you think, you'll find out.
A beautiful angel behind her soft tint of gloom.

It was Friday, about five in the afternoon,
She showed up; I almost shocked myself.
She looked prettier than ever yet vanished, too soon.
Was I dreaming? She seemed real, herself.

What a beauty, what a smoothness!
God, how I wish to talk to her!
She didn't see me, but it's ok; I saw her!
I could tell it's an angel because my weekend was happiness!

Let me describe my angel

Like a dawn observed on a mountain top,
So is the beauty of my angel.
Like a scent of flower on a spring drop,
So is the fragrance of my angel.

A young gazelle flowing so swiftly;
What a scene, what an enjoyment when she walks.
From left to right, a perfect swing so lovely.
The melody in her voice goes out like a symphony when
she talks,
What a sound behind her look, so dolly.

Her eye, when she looks at me,
Is like a cool shower on a hot summer day.
Her smile, when she does it to me,
Is like a warm jacket on a freezing winter day.

Ho! How I love your world, beautiful angel.
Please invite me in, or stop me before I take you as my
angel.

Out of my heart

If I were a King,
I would've conquered many kingdoms
To cover you with silver and gold,
I would've offered the lands of my spoil
As a dowry for your hand
And I would've seated you at my right
As the most beautiful queen on earth.
I am descendent of a King
And believe me when I say,
"Your splendor is of the level of a queen."
I mean that.

I fell again

This was the love of my childhood
To become dove of my manhood.

Deep in love, I was with you,
Still to solve, I stand with you.

These words from you, and it recalled my love.
These memories of you, and I befall in love.

We have grown since, but I did not outgrow it by an inch.
I thought it was gone since, so I did not anticipate that
pitch.

Splendid were you when I perceived you as a child
And beautiful are you today as I receive you in the wild.

I would recall what we have in common without a word
from mammon.
You should call the fall of the handsome without a sound
of cannon.

Sing to me, bird of paradise, so I will hymn to you, angel on
my side.
Pray for me on the outside, so I may free myself on the
inside.
Or write to me on the safe side, so I can reply to the sister of
my soul, on the bright side.

I finally found my soul mate

She is the one, the girl of my youth.
I felt it strong when she sounded it out of her month.
Sea of the one, Perl of my tooth.

    I am the one, who gave her the first kiss.
    The time was gone, who had her to miss.

I called upon my mate, the sister of my soul
I fall upon the rate, the mystery of my goal.

    She called mine sister; she waited, for me she called out.
    Recalled mine twister; she weighed, for me she was
    about.

For years you've waited for your King.
Give me your hand, sweet, beauty of queen.
Live gear you've painted for my ring.
Leave me your sand, tweet, sweetly off screen

    I would share my love and tear
    To the dear heart of yours to bear.

Let's ride the horizons of the Universe,
For the eternity is ours to rehearse.

    Let's love and romanticize again
    For the rest of our time is to gain.

Splendid creature

She is a sweet heart.
The most beautiful woman in the world.
She does not know it;

> Sweet behind quiet,
> Thin without diet,
> She is the one, the mate of my one.
> She is pretty, the daughter of the One.

I thirst for her romance;
If she only knew how lovely that sounded.
I thirst for her cadence;
If she only knew how heavy that pounded.

> Darling, I am in love; sing to me, and I'll be turned on.
> Darling, you call me King, bring it on to me and I'll call
> you queen,
> Darling, I am your cove; wring it to me, and I'll be busted
> on.
> Darling, you call my ring; bring it on to see how I am
> seen.

Stay with me, so together we shall be.
Hold on me, so forever we shall flee.

Pure love, eternal

Let me share my joy of love for you;
Because you are my toy of more to do.

Your entity befalls my mask;
Eternity recalls my lack.

A day like a thousand,
A say like a laugh sound.

Darling, I solved you, from now on,
Forever more, I lay it down.

From the earth of your lips, a glimpse,
To the heavens of your hips, to glimpse,

My queen, let it be, love, always, from within the core.

Colorful lover

Her teeth are like snow dipped into honey.
Her eyes are like rubies immerged into crystal water.
Her skin is like a baby's complexion, I could follow her
curves so softly.

> Her voice reminds me of a morning bird
> Singing to me a melody that I've never heard.

Her lips are like rose petals
Giving me the nectar of her sweet teeth.
Her hips are like water melons
Dangling to give the fruit of a life worth.

> Her entire self is a creature, the missing rib, the soul,
> The entire self of a creature, the colorful sister of my soul.

Love is never tired

Can you feel that warm touching over your hand? Since love
does not retire
My hand will be a warm blanket over yours; tender desire.
Can you see that burning fire of happiness in your heart?
Since love does not have a wire
Your heart like mine, together would merge on fire.
Can you hear the whispering of the wind on this road of love
flowing with desire?
A touch of your skin like a kiss to wire,
My eyes would tell you how much love is worth to revive
that fire.

A sacrifice of love! A wish like a prayer

Time is getting heavier and heavier
So far from you, the feeling is getting lighter.
I have met a lady, she is the other.
I felt weaker as she got closer.
I didn't want to, but the desire. It was getting louder.
I almost touched her; hugged her; kissed her and more. I
almost did it with her!
But almost! Just almost! Nothing deeper.
Because I have wondered about that fever
How should I prove you my love if I'm a swindler?
How should we preserve our love unbroken if I'm a
deceiver?
How can I be a man if I'm a quitter?
For a man isn't the one who waited so long before crossing
the river;
But the one who waited very long without going in; that's a
good soldier.
Since I didn't do it, here is what I'm going to tell you, my
lover;
Thus far I didn't do it because I love you; my heart to you
forever!

Nothing but love

Forget about everything.
Time and space do not matter anymore,
For where there is love
There is faith. Worry about nothing;

    With faith there are possibilities.
    See, love overcomes obstacles.

Just open your heart,
Let me in.
Just observe my art,
Let me sing.

    Let me love and be loved
    Let me move and be moved.

I can't promise to be harmless,
But I can promise to be sensible.
I can't promise to be flawless,
But I can promise to be humble.

    So let me know what you say,
    Oh pretty one, when I say,
    You and I with Christ, together for an eternity.

Back again

Lady Angelika,
On the days of Chaka,
Kingdoms would've been your backa!

Tell me, beauty of my youth,
Sweetness of my tooth,

Tell me how the Mighty One
Could've created such a being like the one?

A voice like a thousand birds,
A feather like a lovely nest
A gaze like sandy diamonds.

Why don't we trade jewels?
My flame for yours
And my manhood for your stones!

Backa *(Bwamu, African)*: Outfit.

Sleeping love

A simple look
And my soul shook.
I saw her book,
I bit the hook.

But who is this precious?
From inside and out, I love her.
How could I be cautious?
From a far distance, I called her.

She looked, but nothing.
She saw nothing in me.
Then I shouted, "Can't you see?"
"Sorry, not a thing!"

Years went by, then I called again.
Maybe time would've washed my pain.
But, again, I was left in the rain!

I can see, but she can't. What is it then?
Why couldn't this love go away, why stay dormant?
Yes, I tried to blow it off so often,
But that flame only grew from moment to moment!

Finally, I went to the Master, her God.
And He told me, "Tell her, 'I shall show her if she asks,
'Tell her to close her eyes and not look on your masks.
'Tell her to feel and see without looking on your mud!'"

Three signs I ignored,
four deeds opened my eyes

For a long time you kept on telling me,
"Move on with your life!" That was the first sign; now I see.
For quite a time you were cold towards me,
No more, "I love you." That was the second sign, now I see.
For a hard time you kept on denying me,
"We are not soul-mates!" That was the third sign, now I see.

You did tell me, now I realize; now I see.
That was the first deed that opened my eyes.
I couldn't comfort you anymore; now I see.
That was the second deed that opened my eyes.
You couldn't express your feelings anymore; now I see.
That was the third deed that opened my eyes.
You counted me as nobody, now I see.
That was the fourth deed that opened my eyes.

For years I tried to lead you into softness,
So hard did I try, but no way did you get it.
For years I tried to show you fellowship and godliness,
So painful did it feel, but no way did you understand it.
For a long time I thought you knew love and selfishness,
So depressed was I, but no way did you receive it.

I'm not angry at you, neither am I blaming you.
No! I am angry at myself for being so naïve,
May God help me forgive myself and forgetting you.
Yes! Now I understand that it is time for me to leave.
No need of crying and no sense to arguing, "Good bye!
But I did love you."

Stop hurting me

These words I'm about to write will pain me,
They will pain me to the tear;
But I have to say it and then cry to be set free.
I will say it with no fear.

Truly, you hurt me more than anybody else could!
Truly, you let me down more than anybody else should!
And it hurts more to know that you don't care!
It breaks my heart in pieces to see that you have no
feelings to share!

I tried to hurt you back,
But I couldn't! That man in me is no more.
I tried to turn my back,
But I couldn't! My heart is trapped to its core.

Before, I would've shaken you off like a bird.
I tried that, too, but it backfired!
Now here am I, crying and soaking my eyes up like a
nerd!
Because that love for you can't be fired!

Deep in my heart, I can feel that root.
Pulling on it would hurt me even more.
Going to another one is neither on my foot.
Hurting you would hurt me even more.

Why can't I just forget you?
Why can't I just harm you back?
Am I too weak or am I too deep in love with you?
Is my heart too soft to the point of holding back?

I can't stop myself from doing you good!
I can't withhold my heart from falling in love!
Maybe is my heart just calling his soul-mate, his dove?
Maybe do I still thirst after the love of yours, my food?

Maybe I should go back to what I do best?
To love you and forgive you, or to forgive you and love you!
To be myself and forget about the rest!

As of you! For love's sake, I don't want to harm you! Then stop doing so!
I love you out of a pure heart!
I might be naïve, but not stupid also!
Keep it up and one day you'll receive your part!

Enough is enough

I don't feel like talking to you anymore.
I thought about letting you know,
"Until you humble yourself, to treat me as a husband, to the core,
I would not heed you any longer! No! I won't, not now."

This time, figure it out yourself; think!
For years I gave you my love, I made you feel like a queen.
You abused it; you thought my heart can't blink!
Now, I am revolted, I will be the worst you've ever seen.

Who do you think you are! How dare you talk to me like a kid!
"Do me the favor of answering me!"
Who do you think you are talking to? A boy? Someone stupid?
"Oh, I am too precious, he cannot leave me!"

You think so? You wish! We shall see!
I would drop you in a heart bit! I don't care anymore!
I spoiled you to that point! My bad; let me get off my knee!
I will teach you a lesson! And if you refuse, I will leave you at the seashore!

Be of good cheer; I am not cheating on you!
Neither did I met anybody else! I am doing better than that!
I am preserving myself for Another! Not for you!

Truly I am not making enough
To take care of you.
Truly I am homeless and you can laugh,
But my dignity, my manhood is not up to you!

I don't need you to call and check on me,
Worry about yourself!
I don't need you either to say, "Talk to me!"
No! I have a mind to decide that myself!

I don't even care if you care not!
I don't even care if you love me not!
You abused my precious love, treating me as if I were full
of wine.
So let me pick my precious back, since you want to act
like a swine.

Song of love to dissolve

Darling you're sad,
Please don't be;
I'm feeling bad,
Let's be free.

    You know darling, one day in the days of bee,
    Together we'll be, better days we'll see.
    A long life we'll see, or to eternity we'll flee.
    Darling, my honey, will see, in love forever would she.

Life is hard, you know; but knowledge in pain you'd sow.
Pain in your heart to blow, wisdom in your future to flow.
Darling, the day at hand will come,
Forever, together at hand at home.

    But darling in pain is in love,
    Her heart and body say "Now".
    Darling, in pain you should know,
    The decision comes from above.

Darling, my queen in love, shining my scene to solve.
My queen, my love, my dove; in love my heart to resolve,
With part of me in love, your root in me will evolve.

Tears of a poet

The world shall see our rise,
Darkness shall free our prize.

It might not be today. It might not be tonight.
But on a time of a day, our time shall free the flight.

Today I cried, yesterday alone.
The day is mined, the past, it is gone.

My pain, your rain is a dime.
My gain in pain is a prime.

Please let me cry, for the tears within my heart.
Please let me fly, for the gear within my cart.

Work alone, I did. Loneliness and shame, I dine.
Heart of one, I bid. Faithfulness, she came in mine.
It is done; we did. Happiness and fame to shine.

To my lost dove

My heart is still crying tonight
The pity of losing the fight.
Poet of love, hard love to solve.
I lost my love, pain to dissolve.

But who needs to hear that? That tear of the poet in love.
Yet, who needs to cheer that? That sear of the sunset
involve.

My tear is dropped in silence, I must avoid some violence.
My beard has not passed guidance, I must convey the
sentence.

From here on, I shall keep my pen on.
From thereon, I shall peak my tent on.

But tonight, let me cry; maybe tomorrow, I shall be dry.

So painful

I have loved you without reserve
To feel so much pain on the curve.
Am I angry at you? No! I think I failed.
I was not able to guide you on the field.

   I lost you, but I still love you.
   In my pain, I don't want you,
   But in my heart, I still need you.

In your face, I hold back,
But, alone, I cry on my back.

   I cannot understand. It is so hard and complicated.
   I cannot hold my stand. It is so far unsolicited.

Please do something, don't let it go away this way.
Help me, because my pain still won't go away my way.

Goodbye

A day has gone.
My tears won't stop.
For love alone,
My pain won't drop.

My heart won't let go,
But my pain says, "Suffer!"
My soul, yet says no,
But my pride says, "Get her!"

I had promised myself not to fall in love,
But here am I, tackled by surprise.
And here am I receiving a prize:
You and me are no more lovers, and above.

Be safe, and thank you for when we were involved.

Love equation

Every day, I try to convince myself that I don't want you.
Every night, I think about you before I go to bed
And all the time, I find myself drawn closer and closer to
you.

> Cutting you off my life would be same as cutting off half
> of myself;
> I would hurt myself more than I would hurt you.
> Likewise, you would hurt yourself more than you would
> hurt myself.

By trying to teach you something, I ended up teaching
myself.
I tried hard not to miss you, but I am tired of crying. Shame
on me.
I tried hard to be the toughest, but love has softened myself.
You've hurt me to the extreme, I cried, and then I wanted
you away from me.

> I tried hard not to care about you, but I am hurting for
> loving you.
> You are pain onto me, but at the same time, you are vital
> to me.
> I tried hard not to want you, but I am in pain for needing
> you.

I have found nothing making you worthy of bearing my love,
But I have also found out that you need nothing to bear my
love.
Can you really understand my pain? Do you feel the same?
That pain telling me that I am truly in love. Can you feel the
same?

It was, once

She left me yesterday, the pain is gone.
I felt it the other day, another to come.

Cry, and again, cry to purge my pain; the love of one.
Weep, and again, weep; and not faint; that love is done.

Like a nightmare, she said enough, "I want out"
I wonder if she ever loved me.
She gave up, she can't wait anymore; she bailed out.

Look! I heard of a love that never gives up.
Of an affection that suffers all and stands up.
Of a care that overshadows self and cheers up.

Have you? I am in pain, but why should I say it?
Do you care? My heart was reduced to pounder
"Breaking it" is not the word, you crunched it and then blew
on it.

Sadly, I watch you go,
Boldly, you can say so.

With tears in my eyes, I picture you in another arm.
No more would you tweet to me,
No more would you cherish me,
Just let me cry before the calm.

Out of my pain, during the rain, you quit,
You were the same coming again to tweet.

I can hope, but can I take it again?
I can float, but can I land it again?
So good bye and please remember me sometimes.

Wipe your tears off. It's over

Life years in past;
Thrive dear at last.

Look not onto the day of pain
Cook something for the day of rain.

A day like today
In a short tomorrow to come.
A say like yesterday
In more tomorrow at home.

Your tear of sorrow,
You shall remember no more.
Your dear will follow,
You shall forever color.

In a quick day like today
We shall be reunited.
In a picked day may I say
We shall say "We've survived!"
Just like a quick say, day by day.

I miss you; I can't enjoy it without you

My heart is crying.
I am sad.
My love is soaring.
I am mad.

Goods and money can't give me joy!
I have been receiving manifold;
Yet, I can't tell what is worth it to enjoy!

Only God can fill that whole in my heart,
I am feeling so sad.
His love only masters the beauty of that art.
I am feeling so bad.

Even if I become famous; making millions of dollars.
All would be vanity if I don't have God by my side.
Even if they show me on TV like a strong pillar.
It would mean nothing to me if I don't have you as my
bride.

Lord forgive me for my sadness,
Thank you for Your blessing.
But only the one of she and I uniting
Would give me tears of happiness.

She suffered along with me,
Side by side, we fought together.
Could I enjoy these blessings without her?
No! Together and happy should we be.

Today, alone and separated, tears of sadness do we have. Tomorrow, together and reunited, tears of happiness shall we shave.

Puzzled up

I've fought many battles in various realms.
I've stood up against mighty beings in heavenly realms;

 Yet, I feel so shaky in the realm of love;
 I feel as nervous and shy as a dove.

Who are you to make me feel like this?
Who is this bringing trouble upon a king like this?

 What is it that I see?
 A shadow of a Queen?
 What is it that I flee?
 A reflection of my scene?

So who are you to shake my bones of love?
Are you the one, the missing rib on my side?
Am I lost? Confused, maybe, toward such equation to solve?

Quiet stranger

About a year ago,
I first saw her walking to and fro.

I wondered as I looked at her,
"What a pretty butterfly in wander!"
But I kept it to myself and didn't tell her.

A few months went by;
Here was I, yet shy.

Oddly, I overheard a sumptuous voice one day.
I wondered, "Whose voice is this to cut me off my way?"
It was her, again! Now, what can I say?
Something inside me said then, "Why go away?"

Yet, I kept it to myself;
Maybe the wind would've blown it off my shelf.

Then a few weeks went by
And here was I, still shy.

Oddly, again, one day, of my way, she came across.
Surprised, I said, "Hi!" as if I were a boss.

Then an unexpected thing happened:
She replied, "Hi!" I was strengthened.

I said, "How are you?"
She said, "Good! How are you?"

It was so brief and quick
That the moment didn't stick.

But afterwards, I was under the charm;
Something in me called back the harm.

I wondered, "What is it about her?
"It is as if Something were driving one to the other!"

So, daringly, I learn to talk to her more and more.
I found out on the way that I wasn't as shy as before,
But a dormant flame was candling from within my core;
I know that I might get hurt, but I have to go to that shore.

Then again, one thing remains that I wonder,
"Is she alone? Is she taken? Is it settled forever?
"How would she react if I were to challenge her?
"What would she say if I were to dare her to give me her
number?"

Fever

My body is neither hot nor cold,
But the temperature within me is many degrees fold.

Fever!

Here she comes, svelte, smooth and as colorful as a bee;
And there she goes, svelte, smooth and as beautiful as I see.

Fever!

If I could, I wouldn't blink from that sight.
What a flower, what a fragrance; not too heavy, not too light.

Fever!

This is fever when she becomes
Color of rose
And this is fever when she breathes;
I think I'll overdose.

Fever!

Call my name and I'll be hotter;
Give me your hand
And I'll give you some land;
Sing my name and I'll be lover.

Fever!

For tomorrow to come, I'll see her
In forever to sum in fever.

Precious

Her hair is like an exotic flowers;
Scent of many roses adorned with many colors.

Her cheeks are like firm apples;
Tender petals, smooth leather that sizzles.

Her smile is a drizzle
Of rain of joy and giggle.

Her quietness is a mystery
Of one who learned in beauty.

Her line is a crown
Bejeweled with colors of the dawn;
She is a jewel of a kingdom of renown.

Refreshing refuge in the desert;
Missing her is like missing an oasis;
Her words are like fresh fruit for dissert.

Many times, I came close to asking,
"When is it, precious ruby?"
Many times, I came close to saying,
"Let have a date, glowing firefly!"

Lesson

This was easy to say,
But so hard to apply;

A piece of bread with peace of mind
Is better than a piece of steak with fear behind.

This was the day
To learn it all the way.

My feelings were hurt,
My pride was broken.
My goal were to flirt,
My heart was shaken.

I always stood up for the prettiest ones;
Thin, quiet and desirable ones,
So how painful was it to break myself down to the other
ones.

What a belief I found in iniquity;
Focusing on a shape was so easy
That looking beyond it became lowly.
But what a relief I found in humility

To pick one, wise and fairly looking, woman
With compassion
Over one, fine and pretty looking, woven
With rebellion.

The last dance

When I move my right foot,
She moves her left foot.

> When I move to my right side,
> She moves to her left side.

When I lift up my right hand,
She lifts up her left hand.

> When I move forward,
> She moves backward.
> When I move backward,
> She moves forward.

When I swing,
She swings
When I turn,
She turns
When I stop,
She stops.

> When I smile,
> She smiles.
> When I laugh,
> She laughs.
> When I cry,
> She cries.

So I wonder,
"Who is this like my mirror?"

And she said,
"I am your half, your female side
"And you're my male side!"

So I said,
"Are we hearing the same melody?"
And she said,
"Yes, my dear! What a symphony!"

We are on one accord in the spirit,
Under the same rhythm of the Spirit.
From our spirits to shine,
From her soul to mine.

Fervent white Agapa

Freshness of the godly

This is only the beginning. The worst is to come. Yet speechless against the event; in the silence, we communicate the chaos, one to the other, "It is happening. We are the generation appointed to the apocalypse."

The foundations of the world are shaking. The entire system of mankind is collapsing. Our civilization is barely standing. Only those with their heart set upon the upcoming age will prevail: it is time to wake up.

A metaphysical concept, that is to face a mathematical enigma of God.

Wisdom is a gift from God that age has nothing to do with.

There is nothing more honorable than to give a smile, some hope, or peace, onto ones' life. This also reflects the fruit of the Spirit. Through the joy of others, you should know if you're fulfilling the will of The Father.

If you love, love with a pure heart, without holding back. Because that is how our Father loves us.

Fasting will make one appear physically weak, but spiritually he shall be strong.

Fasting is not reserved to an elite of Christians; rather to a Christian who will make himself an elite by fasting.

Many times scientists had tried to contradict God by blaming Nature instead. They should've known that nature itself is controlled by God.

We should neither use science, nor technology, nor philosophy to try to prove the existence of God, but rather acknowledge the fact that they have been given to us to understand creation itself: we should consider all of it as a proof of God's Omniscience.

Should science be opposed to God? Shouldn't we analyze it better? What if science and Bible were both right? In one hand we would have God telling us what happened with the Bible and on the other hand He would show us how it happened with science. It is worth it to give it a thought.

The world does its best to deny God, yet they refer to the seven days standard set by God in the Bible. How awkward is that?

A worldly man would dump you after uncovering the dirty side of yours, but a godly man would love you still, because he understands that we are not perfect.

God will always bless us despite what we do! Not doing right or wrong in our lives has nothing to do with the blessing of God. He makes it rain on the wicked as well as on the godly and that makes of His blessing a gift up to Him to give! However, one would lose his salvation by not doing what's right!

From time to times, things seem to be confusing; life appears to be unsettling or disturbing and we end up feeling trouble-minded or lost. Still, we have to hang on, because unconsciously we are still moving according to the perfect plan of God.

I am a mighty warrior of God, talented and gifted indeed; within me lives a King, within my hand resides a power that can overthrow kingdoms, and with my month I can speak things into existence. With the authority given to me through Christ Jesus, I profess and believe that Christ is the LORD. With Him on my side I am a conqueror, victorious; I am an over-comer, unshakable. I will take back what the enemy has stolen from me and by the guidance of the Living Spirit I will possess the kingdom given onto me.

Complain not when you receive a little, but thank the LORD so He will provide some more.

We have the tendency sometimes to pray for money. Instead of a fish, shouldn't we pray about knowing how to fish? If we succeed, wouldn't it count money in the equation?

A doctor can find a cure to a disease indeed, but healing comes from God.

The Hand of God is beautified through contentment and His goodness is beheld with the eye of the humble one.

Which one is your priority; the Father or His blessings? If it's the Father, know then that everything shall come along with Him. But if it's His blessings, then know that you shall have none of it!

The conquest of your heart and soul are a priority to God more than blessing you!

Notice: when things go wrong in life, then comes time of humility. The more you'll resist, the more God will resist you.

Do not look upon the mighty giants living in the land to worry your soul, but rather look upon The Mighty Hand of God beside you to strengthen your heart; and always remember that struggle might be yours, but the fight is the LORD's and your victory is imminent.

I have a treasure that no one can steal. It is called "Joy!" I have a fire that no water can contain. It is called Spirit. And I have some Water that no death can handle. It is called Christ! Put all together and you'll find the recipe of life.

The blessings of the LORD come with The Morning Star, but the eyes of man decide to go blind on them!

In tough times, I wonder, "Why is it that I suffer, if God is with me?" Then I realize afterward that I've survived a tribulation, and My LORD was The One who preserved me.

Help me, if you can, the way you can; but remember, the LORD will raise me higher, if you don't.

The peace and love in Christ is better than the pleasures of this world!

My God is so Mighty that the Universe cannot contain Him, but He is so lovely that your heart would fit Him.

From micro to macro, He is omnipresent. From tinny to mighty, He is omnipotent; and from limited to infinite, He is omniscient. No wonder, He is The Almighty!

Don't try to be perfect, none of us can; just be yourself, natural. Also, understand that sin is in our nature and doing our best to avoid sinning is our daily struggle.

An ungodly loved one can be as dangerous as an enemy. He will drive you in front of other gods and while thinking that he is protecting you or blessing you, he will be allying you with the evil side and pouring curses onto your life. His love is true indeed, but misguided for sure.

The conquest of a new land; a new territory to relax or call, "Home"; on Earth, we go after pieces of dirt; in heaven we shall go after pieces of heavens, the Universe. One thing remains however, is that you must be one of us!

In winter times, the cold weather coming through makes us forget all about the heat of summer times; in summer times likewise. It is as if the other season had not existed. Thus is the way of God's Hand in one's life. It makes us forget all about the past trials and tribulations over the enjoyment of His blessing. We should remember those days however, and fear the LORD forever!

Forgive me if I am hard heated sometimes; just work with me while the LORD is working on me. He had created me that way and knows about it, too; yet, He would not stop blessing me for His love's sake.

The beautiful life is the reflection of God presence in one's life.

When God bound someone for success, what he does would not matter; success will follow. On the other hand, if one's time has not yet come, standing still would be best thing to do.

So you think you've successful because you're smart, or healthy because you "eat healthy", or live longer because you're "good"? Think again! And, don't take what was given by grace for granted!

Even cats and gods get along. Even man and God sand the land. But man to man don't hand to hand!

It doesn't matter if one's theory or concept of heaven is a bit blurry. What is important is that he sets his heart upon It (The Kingdom of God). Truth will be reveal once there; until then, dreaming is a freedom to enjoy on our way of seeking God in spirit and truth.

If you love money more than God, you will lose your life. If you love your husband or wife more than God, you will lose your heart. But if you love God more than anything, you will keep everything.

Enjoy life while you can; be content with what you have and look up to the Father for a better future.

You can take a man out of the ghetto, but you can't take the ghetto out of a man. His appearance will change indeed, but his habits will remain; still, whatever is impossible with man, is possible with God.

Be grateful for the way you are; you're just perfect as you are. Indeed, if I were but one inch taller, I would've missed heaven by that much!

Let him know, him who tries to resist love, that he is also trying to resist God; because God is love.

Wait for a dark clear night, then lift up your eyes to the heavens and then count the stars in the firmament; if you can count them, then you would grasp a glimpse of how much love He has for you.

As soft as a touch of a cool summer breeze; as warm as a fire heat under a frigid winter snow; and as splendid as a knight coming back from victory; thus is the care of our God for us.

Sadness

Helpless under the sun of wickedness,
Hopeless under the pain of homelessness
On skid Row where madness and craziness rhymes with
wilderness.
I wonder how long will it be? I am so restless!
Looking for help and mercy. I will call He who is not
heartless.
Cast away, looking down on, lower than a dog and so
useless.
How could they give a home to an animal, but the streets to
the homeless.
I only expected the left over not to be so lawless.
I will cry out more onto Him from the darkness.
Before sinking into hopelessness
I will remember that a word from Him can change sadness to
happiness.

He is, God

I have heard of It before.
Many had talked about It before.
I have read It from the Bible before.

Since that day You kept on blessing me.
I have sinned, but You still poured It out on me.

Since that day, I wondered;
Since that grace I squandered!

Is it true? I mean, is Your Love overpowering sin?
Is it true that even sin wouldn't stop You? Both wide and
thin?

I have sinned, I'm insane, still it won't stop Your Hand!
Forgive me for what I am, let me not fall out from Your
sweet Hand!
Even now I'm still grasping the beginning of It,
That Love so sweet and merciful. I feel so ashamed of
receiving It.

I feel so unworthy of It that my heart gets melted away.
LORD, let me just be with You, allow me to adore You
just one more day;
A day that would last an eternity in Your day.
Close Your eyes on my iniquities, cleanse me to prepare
me for Your Way.

My eyes have seen You, Mercy above mercies,
Sweetness above sweetness,
Love above loves.

My ears have heard Your voice, Softness above softness, Warmth above warmth, Loftiness above loftiness, Mightiness above mightiness; be glorified God, kindness above kindness!

I have heard about The Mighty Warrior

On earth He was the Son of a mighty one,
He was the Son of David.
In heaven He is The Son of The Mighty One,
He is the Son of God.

My tongue has tasted his care,
He is The Provider.
My inheritance comes from His share,
He is The Richest Brother.

My pain has called His tears,
He is The Father.
My armor comes from His gears,
He is The Most High General of the soldier.

My lost has caught His attention,
He is The Keeper.
My brokenness is His admission,
He is The Potter.

My mind has sought His vision,
He is The Counselor.
My sins had proven His perfection,
He is The Strongest Warrior.

My life has been His choice,
He is The Creator.
My ears had heard His voice,
He is The Shepherd, The Greatest Mentor.

My heart has loved His mercy,
He is The Most Merciful Lover.
My eyes had seen His Glory,
He is The Most Trusted Power.

    My flesh has felt His presence,
    He is The living One; The Healer.
    My soul has experienced His Grace,
    He is The Most Tender Guider.

My weakness has exercised His Strength,
He is The Mighty of all mightiness.
My filthiness has confirmed His Wealth,
He is The King of the homeless.

    I have tested the warmth of His arms,
    He is The Warmth of the mother.
    I have sung the songs of His psalms,
    He is The Voice of the singer.

I have breathed off His Blow,
He is The Breath of life.
I have lived off His flow,
He is The Brightness of the sunshine.

    I came to know Him and found out that He is what I
    needed;
    I came to seek Him and found out that He is sweeter than
    a woman;
    Stronger than a lion and swifter than the wind, He is what
    I wanted.

His eyes give you happiness,
His smile gives you healthiness,
His Voice resurrects and gives you worthiness,
And His kiss keeps you in holiness.

A day with Him and you wonder if you have ever lived,
A sight of Him and you wonder if have ever seen beauty,
A word from Him and you wonder if you have ever been
healed,
Some love from Him and you wonder if you have
remained a baby.

His Name is The Eternal of the Armies.
His width is spread beyond the universe.
His brightness shines greater than all the suns.
He is King Jesus, handling galaxies like little countries.

Shame

I am ashamed of my deeds.
The LORD of heavens sees.
Under the roof of that seed,
The LORD still provides my need.

    I first thought He would punish me,
    But my God of forgiveness forgave what I couldn't see.
    I tried to walk by the law,
    But my iniquity and default, He saw.

I thought I could be righteous,
But what I call righteousness, to Him, is filthy and
ungracious.
I thought I was good,
But what I call "good", to Him, is dirt, mud under the hood.

    The big things I thought I did were little in His sight.
    The big work I thought worthy wasn't counted as light.
    So I thought I was lost:
    I cannot make it, I am even unworthy of paying such a
    cost.

Then He told me:
"Not by law, but by faith.
Believe and your sins, no more will they be."

I did not; He did it

Some people call me saint,
Others call me angel.
But calling me so could become my tower of Babel.
I consider myself, in His sight, less than an ant.

> I haven't done anything worthy of being a saint,
> Neither have I done any work worthy of being an angel.
> By grace I was granted this channel.
> By faith I have received that tent.

"One of us" is my identification.
"Unworthy" I call myself when I face temptation.
"Save me" I cry out when I face sinfulness.
"Mercy" I cry for when I face the consequences.

> Grateful was I, when He covered my sin.
> Joyful was I, when He called me in.
> Humiliated, was I when He closed His eyes on my bin.

If, by myself, I were to stand,
My strength wouldn't carry me.
With grace and mercy He holds my hand:
He made me as such as they say of me.

From my heart, to my mind, to Him

How can one describe Someone above words?
How can one picture Someone above description?
Wouldn't he only say what he remembers?
Wouldn't he put it in words of explanation?

His eyes are like an infinite ocean of love
Mingled with kindness, joy, peace
And everything that is good and much much more.

His smile is like a sizzling dust of diamonds
Mingled with light and colors.

His breath is like the freshness of oxygen.
It's a fountain of living waters.
His voice is like many waters
Sounding like melody, clear and soften.

His word is authority
And flows with harmony.

His work is mighty,
A pure demonstration of wisdom.
His wrath is calamity,
A pure condemnation, a doom.

If heavens were only about Him
Still it would've been worth it going.
If eternity were only to gaze at Him
Still it would've been worth it lasting.

Yet, no one will ever have enough of Him eternally.
If you've ever seen Him, you'll understand.
You'll stop everything just to sight His beauty.

Love above all

When I saw His glory,
My life stopped.
And then I saw His beauty,
And everything else stopped

    Just to adore Him;
    Nothing else mattered.
    I only wanted to stay with Him
    Nothing else counted.
    Nothing else was like Him.

Live and love Him and nothing more.
Loving my life was no more,
Everything was then about Him and for Him
From eternity past to eternity to come.

High above

He brought me high, out of the night,
High above the human sight.
I marveled. Still, this was light.

He let me reach higher, above what the human mind could
dare.
I was speechless.
I was on fire beyond anything I could share.

I kept silent, then I couldn't hold it,
So I said it; I beautified It!

And mankind marveled. Still, this was nothing
To compare with what I saw.
Just see It and feel It; still, you won't understand a thing!

Son of God

Knowing that I am unrighteous,
Knowing that I am a sinner,
You still refer to me as righteous.
You still refer to me as saint and believer.

Humbly I'll come to You,
Shamefully I'll confess my sins to You.
With an opened heart I'll talk to You.
For Your grace and loving-kindness, I'll adore You.
You are God. I did not deserve You,

Many times I have hurt You,
Yet, You remained forgiving and faithful;
I can't help but to praise You.

You've revealed Yourself to me.
Through the eye of Your Love
I am made perfect. I am Your son.
Away from You I find no peace,
But You still preserve me from my vice.

Close to You I can see my iniquity,
But You clean me up and dress me up so nicely.

No words can describe You.
My heart shall forever thank You.

You are a Jewel more precious than life
And more beautiful than a diamond.
You are The Brightest Light that could ever shine
And The Warmest Love, most Colorful and beyond.

Allow me to dwell in Your house,
Give me Your heart so I can be more like You.
Shine on me, so Your Spirit will live within me,
Let me not drift away from You,
But guide me under the sweet sound of Your Voice.

Heaven

It is where reality takes place,
A place that my soul longs for;
The kingdom of Him that I adore.

For years I searched and researched,
Making note, writing books and theories.
I looked and observed,
Thinking and meditating from countries to cities.

At last it was revealed to me;
I dropped my pen.
A blast I received in me;
I saw Heaven.

The Shekinah Glory was there
And love waves emanated from Her, so pure,

More refreshing than oxygen,
More strengthening than food
And far more pleasurable than sex by ten.

There, is the Home of unconditional love,
The One, the fervent One for one another.
There, is the Home of simplicity and above,
Defiling the laws of physics like a river.

Truth was finally revealed
And looking back to my notes, books and theories
I can see the flaws; I wish to have them sealed,
But again, they were helpful stories.

So let him who seeks The Truth
Be open-minded, flexible and moldable.
Because the day shall come when The Truth
Will defile his concept on his table.

But let him also be humble,
Because Heaven is so simple
That it will not be so impressive when described; if possible.

The New Earth

I saw the new planet.
Nature replaced machine
And wisdom replaced cuisine.
It is a garden of a natural carpet.

    Those living in it possessed a New Mind;
    Rubies, diamonds, all the stones that we consider
    "Precious"
    Had become as nothing; easy to find,
    They became as construction material; not so "Fabulous".

Those living there had a New Currency;
Love became the universal trading coin.
Peace, joy and many more were in the treasury.

    They possessed power and might
    To control things on sight.

They possess wisdom and life
Instead of death and strife.

    The Universe is their limit;
    Eternity is their time.
    Galaxies are their mansions to sit;
    Earth is their prime.

God is their Father;
Angeles are their workers.
Their conscious is together
And their work is for others.

What a sight!
I knitted, "My heart is there, away"
I sighed, "I want to go today
"Or tonight!"

Eternal Life, Eternal Love

Haven't you heard?
How He does whatever He wants?
Haven't you learned?
How He strikes whatever He wants?

Love has no laws and no prison!
Everything has a purpose!
Everything is for a reason!
And nothing is without Love.

Shine forth, you shall do just fine.
Son of God,
Love forth, you shall have no line.

Love is without laws;
There shall be no wrongs.

Conclusion
(Poetry shall never die)

Love like God and Beauty like Divine. Poet of love like poet
of God, I glorify God true love.
By the Divine Goodness
The inspiration is endless
Sometime with sadness
To show how much Love is happiness.

Epilogue

Forgive me if I speak much to your heart, I'm only human. Understand that I seek to nurture your soul, mine as well; I'm only a poet.

About the Author

Dofini Tamini was born in Burkina Faso, West Africa. He started writing poetry at the age of 15 to self published his first poetry book in 2002 in Burkina Faso and in 2004 in France.

He wrote 12 spiritual (gospel) tracts that are published online by **Dofini Unit** (California Non-Profit Organization) **www.DofiniUnit.org.**

From his first book titled **Coming to USA** published in 2010, ***Dofini Tamini*** had not stopped expending his horizon as an author.

For more information about the author, please log on **www. DofiniTamini.com**

From the same author:

Books:
> ***Coming to USA*** (Memoire)
> ***FETH: Celestial Battle*** (Novel – Book 1)
> ***Clash of the Mortals (FETH: Origin)*** (Novel – Book 2)

Poetry book:
> ***Saisons de jesunesse*** (French poetry)

Gospel tracts
(published by Dofini Unit www.DofiniUnit.org):

> ***Deliverance from demons***

> ***Deliverance spiritual prisons***

Alliance with God

From earth to heaven

Life after death

Soul-mates

The secret of fasting

Addiction how to break out of it

The Trinity

The Christian Life

Pray over your place

The rapture, be prepared

Would you like to see your manuscript become a book?

If you are interested in becoming a PublishAmerica author, please submit your manuscript for possible publication to us at:

acquisitions@publishamerica.com

You may also mail in your manuscript to:

**PublishAmerica
PO Box 151
Frederick, MD 21705**

We also offer free graphics for Children's Picture Books!

---

www.publishamerica.com

CPSIA information can be obtained at www.ICGtesting.com
Printed in the USA
BVOW05*0630110615

404064BV00001BA/1/P